Genre Writing

by Patricia La Barbera

Dedicated

to

beginning writers

who feel like

avalanche victims

Contents

Introduction   *1*

One
What's the Difference?
Genre versus Literary   *3*

Two
Point of View   *5*

Three
Tense, Narrative, Flashback,
Exposition, and Scene   *11*

Four
Speaking about Dialogue   *17*

Five
Sentence Oomph   *21*

Six

I Screamed When I   *29*
Reread My Book

Seven

Character and Setting   *41*
Description

Eight

Endings and Other
Possible Rejection Culprits   *45*

Nine

Before You Submit...
A Checklist for Genre Writers   *49*

Ten

Websites   *53*

Introduction

Wouldn't it be great to know what editors are searching for before you send in a manuscript? And to learn methods of getting past the publisher's gatekeeper?

By following the conventions, authors aren't as likely to have editors reject their manuscripts after reading just a few paragraphs.

When I first started writing, I remember feeling overwhelmed by information. The chapters in this concise book, especially helpful to a beginner, present a quick guide to improving prose and following genre conventions. However, all writers will likely find some useful instruction.

Most of my writing, editing, teaching, and contest-judging experience relates to genre fiction. Genre works consist of categories such as thriller, horror, romance, mystery, science fiction, and fantasy. I based this book's content on several courses I taught through the Sarasota Editors Association, a group I organized.

Throughout the book, I give examples that highlight many of the elements I often have to revise in clients' manuscripts. The content targets genre categories, but much information can apply to literary writing, too.

Chapter one discusses general differences between literary and genre works. The second chapter covers one of the main reasons editors reject manuscripts—problems with point of view. Other chapters contain topics such as dialogue, strong sentences, word choice, and punctuation.

By using a revision of my mystery novella, I show what belongs in the first sentence and paragraph of a book, as well as on the first page.

The final parts include a writer's checklist and useful websites for writers.

Chapter One

What's the Difference?
Genre versus Literary

First, what is genre? Some examples are horror, romance, mystery, thriller, science fiction, fantasy, and their many subcategories.

The shorthand version of the difference between genre and literary is that genre is all about plot and literary is all about character development. Perhaps emphasis would better describe the difference. A genre book with cardboard characters would bore the reader. A literary work with a weak or nonexistent story arc may not live up to its potential, although literary audiences are also more likely to accept experimental pieces.

Traditional genre books tend to get through the plot in a straight line. Flashbacks aren't taboo, but convention places a special emphasis on propelling the plot forward.

Literary works can take the scenic route. The characters often exhibit much introspection. Flashbacks are common. It's not necessary to propel the plot forward as forcefully.

Genre prose needs three main elements: clarity, power, and transparency. The writing shouldn't have any speed bumps that take the reader out of the story.

With genre categories, authors focus on electric but invisible prose. The writing should entrench the audience in the story rather than call attention to itself or an external narrator. By not reminding readers a writer's telling the tale, an author enhances engagement.

With literary writing, the prose itself becomes an object of focus. Literary authors often examine universal, deep issues, whereas those topics would detract from the plot line of a genre novel.

Chapter Two

Point of View

Third-Person-Limited Deep View

This perspective characterizes the norm for genre prose. With third person the main character (or perspective character) is referred to as he, she, it, or by name.

Examples

He planned to visit Europe in the spring.

She received an interesting letter.

Jeremiah laughed when he heard the joke.

The **limited** aspect pertains to the story's unfolding through the perspective of one character per scene.

Some publishers, especially in the romance category, allow a shift in perspective one or more times in a scene, often specifying the use of an extra space before and after.

Sometimes publishers include point-of-view requirements in the submission guidelines. If not, staying with one perspective per scene maximizes an author's chance of acceptance. With the third-person-limited **deep** point of view, no omniscient external narrator intrudes. Filters such as saw, thought, heard, and felt, aren't used, so the reader can experience the story as closely as possible to the way the character does.

Example of External Narrator

The man saw storm clouds darkening the sky. He heard the thunder and felt the chill around him.

Example without External Narrator

Storm clouds darkened the sky. Thunder roared in the distance, and wind gusts chilled his bones.

Head Hopping

The reader learns the thoughts, feelings, and motives of multiple characters in a scene when an author head hops. Head hopping ranks as one of the major reasons editors reject genre manuscripts.

Example

Why did he have to go to this stupid, boring play? Arnold squirmed in the uncomfortable seat.

Julie glanced at him. If only he wasn't bored. Why did he even agree to attend the theater? He should have just stayed home and watched the baseball game.

It's so labor intensive to fix this problem, especially when the author has difficulty understanding about third-person-limited deep point of view, regardless of revision instructions. Publishers also generalize that if the author doesn't know this important convention, he doesn't know other usual practices. The writer gives the impression of being an amateur, so the editor may feel a lack of trust.

Thoughts

Instead of using italics to show thoughts, have the thoughts part of the third-person perspective. For one thing, italics are speed bumps that distract the reader and more effectively show emphasis (sparingly) or show the first occurrence of a foreign word.

Also it's a point-of-view departure when you write the thought from a first-person perspective. Instead of *I hate that man* or I hate that man, he thought, consider the following: Ted spat on the ground. Evil ran through Jake's veins. Notice how the last example is in third person and without an external narrator. The thought is expressed through Ted's perspective.

An exception to this convention occurs when a character speaks to another character in her mind, for example, *I love you, Bob* or with an interjection, such as *Darn!* or *Ugh!* Use the interjection in italics and then switch back to third person: *Darn!* How would he find the answer?

First Person

Sometimes using first person (I) can be a powerful way to tell a story. It's best to experiment with first person and third person to measure which one would be the best vehicle for telling the tale and the most engaging to your reader.

Second Person

The majority of publishers don't favor use of second person (you). The prose, with its perceived invasive quality, has a tendency to annoy readers.

Example

You go to the store and buy groceries. You leave the store and walk to your car. When you get home, someone's sitting in your living room. You call the police.

Chapter Three

Tense, Narrative, Flashback, Exposition, and Scene

Tense

Although present tense could be used, story-time narrative is usually simple past tense. Using this tense for the main part of the book is a genre convention.

Example

She went to the museum.

Story-time dialogue can be present, past, or past perfect. If a dialogue tag is used, though, the tag is past tense.

Example

"I love going to the museum," she told her friend.

Flashbacks are in past perfect tense when story time is in past tense.

Example

As a young man, he'd lived in Seattle.

Flashbacks

It's best to keep flashbacks short and to a minimum. But if you use a longer flashback, one way to keep the word *had* from becoming annoying is to have two or three verbs in past participle in the beginning and then verbs in simple past. Finish the flashback with two or three verbs in past perfect tense, and then segue with a sentence that smoothly transitions to story time (past).

Example

Here's an example showing story time [past verbs] in brackets, the flashback's *past perfect verbs* in italics, the flashback's <u>past verbs</u> as underlined, and the entire (flashback) enclosed in parentheses:

Eric [reminisced] about his earlier years. (As a young man, *he'd lived* in Seattle. The city *had been* so exciting.) He <u>visited</u> art galleries twice a week. Eric <u>met</u> many interesting professionals. At parties people <u>discussed</u> the latest books. Eric <u>enjoyed</u> the varied cuisines of excellent restaurants.

Even though *he'd loved* his job as an advertising executive, *he'd anticipated* the weekends.) Now he [considered] moving again to Seattle.

Other effective ways of relaying backstory include using dreams and dialogue.

Exposition in Narrative

Using narrative for exposition, which relays background information, results in text people tend to skip over.

Example

Jennifer and Karla had been friends for twenty years. They'd come from a town that had only one stoplight. Jennifer had been studious, while Karla had enjoyed sports. Karla had stolen Jennifer's boyfriend in senior year. Steve wound up leaving Karla and marrying someone else and stayed in the town.

Exposition in a Scene

Relaying backstory in a scene with conflict will more likely maintain reader interest.

Example

Jennifer glared at Karla. "You're still the same sniveling baby you were in first grade."

"Oh yeah, Jen. You always thought you were better than I was. Goody Two-Shoes. Straight-A student."

Jennifer's eyebrows shot up. "Really? How could I possibly think that when perky cheerleader stole my boyfriend in senior year. And maybe if you hadn't, he would have married me instead of Laura after he left you."

"Don't blame me Steve didn't marry you." Karla threw up her hands. "You always said the town was too small for you, that you were itching to go to the big city, and you did. You knew Steve would never leave this place. He's still here."

Chapter Four

Speaking about Dialogue

Don't use barnyard dialogue. Some authors have their characters make all kinds of animal sounds in dialogue tags: barked, cooed, clucked, purred, hissed (especially bad to use without any sibilant sounds), growled, etc.

Although some famous writers use animal sounds and synonyms for the word *said* (see next section), these writers' sales have made them immune to the conventions. It's usually in a not-as-well-known writer's best interest to follow the conventions regarding dialogue tags as well as everything else.

Let them have their *say*. The word *said* disappears in a sentence, and it's to a writer's advantage not to substitute synonyms, such as retorted, proffered, offered, etc. *Whispered* is a word that sparsely used can help writers avoid the —ly adverb *softly*.

Use only needed dialogue tags. Though previous writing styles differed, the trend now involves using tags only when necessary to reveal the speaker. Many times the speaker is obvious, as in question-and-answer-type dialogue.

Example

"I have a lot of questions for you," the detective said.

"Oh yeah?" Tony cracked his knuckles.

"Where were you last Saturday night?"

"At the movies."

"Anyone see you?"

"My friend Joey."

"Can you give me his phone number?"

"Sure."

It's usually preferable to have the dialogue tag at the end of a sentence.

Beats can take the place of tags, too. A beat identifies the speaker with an action. The beat can come before or after the dialogue.

Example

Claire scooped up a few dresses. "I have to try these on."

Example

"I won the contest." Larry beamed.

Note the period rather than a comma at the end of the dialogue.

You can't smile a sentence. And even if writers insist upon getting creative with their dialogue tags, some verbs eliminate the possibility of speech, for example:

beamed
chortled
laughed

giggled

sobbed

breathed

coughed

choked

blushed

hiccupped

However, these verbs could be used as beats.

Don't use hard-to-read dialect. Instead of depicting dialect by spelling phonetically, for example, "Ah gwine t' da fishin' 'ole," set the reader up to imagine an accent or dialect. Use word choice to show regional differences.

Example

When Ruby opened her mouth, magnolias bloomed, and her words moseyed out like molasses.

"Never did have no hankering for strawberry pop." She fanned herself with the Picayune Press.

Chapter Five
Sentence Oomph

Is, are, was, and were constructions can weaken the prose. Compare "She was wearing a suit" to "She wore a suit."

Don't settle for plain vanilla. *There was, there were, there is,* and *there are* constitute bland ways of starting a sentence.

Get active. As a general rule, use active voice, as in the following sentence: The man mailed the letter. The next sentence employs passive voice: The letter was mailed by the man.

Vary sentence and paragraph length. Consider sentence fragments, especially in dialogue, where they add realism to the conversation.

Example without fragments

It just didn't make sense. Aaron had always been a very good driver. According to a recent checkup, he had been in excellent health. The car hadn't had any mechanical problems.

Example with fragments

It just didn't make sense. A good driver in excellent health. A car with no mechanical problems.

Also paragraphs of one or a few words can have strong impact.

The important point of a sentence belongs at the end. A sentence's final part gets the most emphasis because of the pause with the punctuation mark and the space. Compare "She stabbed her with a steak knife" to "She grabbed the steak knife and stabbed her."

Revise sentences that have ending prepositional phrases. Compare "He looked through the rooms of the mansion" to "He explored the mansion's rooms."

Use specific nouns and verbs. Note the difference between these titles:

"A Vehicle Called an Urge"
"A Streetcar Named Desire"

Search for word repetition.
are
began to
could
felt
frowned
had
have to
heard
-ing (for example, *wore* instead of *was wearing*)
is
it
just
look
laughed

-ly adverbs (for example, **really** and ***softly***)
mused
paused
rather
saw
smiled
some
started to
stood
that
then
there
thought
turned
very
walked
was
were
wondered
would

Only use the word *that* if necessary for comprehension. In the sentence "He knows that the mail carrier will deliver the package," the word *that* isn't necessary for the sentence's clarity.

Sparsely use introductory phrases. Note how annoying (and amateurish) the following sentences are: Walking down the street, he saw a suspicious character. Moving at a quick pace, he ducked into a doorway. Waiting until the man went into a store, he then scurried onto the pavement.

Include only necessary punctuation marks. Each punctuation mark calls for some kind of pause or stop, so only use one when the prose requires a pause or stop. Otherwise, the pace slows. It's better to regulate pace by lengthening or shortening sentences.

Don't use !? or !!! or ??? Or any combination thereof. It's amateurish.

Include necessary punctuation marks. Punctuation marks are like traffic signals that help readers maneuver through a sentence.

The following sentence highlights a comma's importance: "Let's eat, Grandma."

Use a serial comma (a comma before the *and* in a series) to avoid sentence-comprehension problems, which could occur in the following example: At the zoo Alexander saw his brothers, apes and hyenas.

Separate independent clauses joined by a conjunction with a comma: We went to the museum, and we ate in its restaurant.

Don't use comma splices. Two sentences have to be separated by a period. The following example features a comma splice: We went to the museum, we ate in its restaurant.

Don't use unnecessary commas. They interfere with the flow of sentences, for example, the two commas in this sentence: But, we went to the store and, then the theater.

It's acceptable to start a sentence with a conjunction. See previous example.

Be wary of using semicolons and colons in genre manuscripts. Many publishers frown on using semicolons and colons in genre (especially in dialogue) unless appropriate for historical fiction.

Punctuating the dialogue of a scholarly or snobbish person would be another exception to the convention.

Chapter Six

I Screamed When I Reread My Book

My explosive reaction upon rereading *The Celtic Crow Murders*, a book I published, may seem extreme, but I realized how much I had to revise. In addition to being an author, I became an editor after I published the book. Below is the original first page with revision ideas following the excerpt.

I'll also discuss what belongs in the first sentence and paragraph of a genre manuscript, as well as on the first page. I revised with these concepts in mind, and I'll include the new text. I think the revision has more suspense, and I hope you agree.

The Celtic Crow Murders, version 1

After all the other mourners had left the funeral home, **1** Larissa stood alone in the room with her dead husband's coffin. **2** She looked at

Aaron's body, dressed in a dark suit. Larissa remembered him in his pilot uniform and **3** could see him smiling before one of their many trips together. **4** She felt grateful that at least she had the travel photographs and the articles **5** she had written; **6** they would help her relive those wonderful times **7** they had shared.

Larissa reminisced for a few moments, but visions of the accident **8** came back to haunt her. **9** Sometimes the images she saw were so vivid, she found it hard to believe **10** that she hadn't been in the car.

It just didn't make sense, **11** she thought. **12** Aaron had always been a very good driver. According to a recent checkup, he had been in excellent health. The car hadn't had any mechanical problems. But the police *had* mentioned a second set of skid marks. She shook her head and bent over to kiss Aaron's cheek. She brushed away a tear that fell on it and then walked **13** slowly into the hall to call her daughter.

Standing in front of an ornate mirror, she **14** woodenly punched in Claire's cell phone number. Then **15** out of the corner of her eye, she saw the reflection of a man holding a dagger and standing about ten feet from the coffin. He **16** was wearing a dark coat and a black ski mask. Larissa would have to walk past the doorway to escape.

17 When Claire answered, she whispered to her, "Call the police and send them to the funeral home. I'll explain later." **18** Larissa ended the call before Claire could ask any questions.

Larissa stood **19** terrified and frozen as she watched the man **20** slowly walk up to the casket. **21** She saw him reach into his coat and draw out a flat hexagonal package, which he placed in the coffin. The man raised the dagger over Aaron's body and made circling motions as he **22** slowly lowered it.

When the tip of the dagger reached the neck **23** area, the man stood still for several minutes, chanting something **25** that Larissa couldn't understand. **26** Suddenly, the man extended his left arm and slashed his palm, **27** allowing the blood to fall toward the head of the casket.

Explanations

1. All the other mourners had left, so the reader knows she was alone. The adjective *dead* is unnecessary.

2, 3, 4, 9, 15. Using third-person-limited deep point of view engages the reader more. Use one perspective character per scene, where possible. The *deep* part of this refers to avoiding filters, such as looked, felt, heard, smelled, etc. These words point to an external narrator. In the first example, perhaps use the following: Aaron's body reposed in a dark suit.

10, 25. Only use *that* when it's necessary for comprehension.

5, 6, 7. Using contractions smoothes out the prose. Characters using contractions in dialogue make the speech sound realistic. Not using contractions would be appropriate to emphasize something or if the character is more formal. Also, number five shows the use of a semicolon, which many genre publishers frown on.

8. The excerpt has many end-of-sentence prepositional phrases. Using them at that location tends to weaken the prose. Also the ending punctuation and the following space emphasize the final words. So try to put the main point of the sentence at the end. Here's a possible rewrite: "...but accident visions haunted her."

12. Sentence variation. Here's a possible revision with effective fragments: "A good driver in excellent health. A car with no mechanical problems."

13, 14, 20, 22, 26. These sentences have −ly adverbs. The excerpt has the word *slowly* three times. It's a better idea to use specific verbs.

16. *Is, are, was,* and *were* constructions tend to weaken the prose. In this example, use *wore.*

17. Better to show Claire's dialogue: "Hi, Mom."

18. The sentence isn't necessary.

19, 20. Revision: "Larissa froze. The man crept up to the casket."

25. The phrase "that Larissa couldn't understand" isn't necessary because "chanting something" suggests the idea. Also the word *that* isn't needed.

26. Suddenly, things aren't so sudden. It's better to just present what happens without prefacing it with *suddenly*, which should have a comma after it, and that slows things down even more.

27. The prose would be stronger with a new sentence, such as "Blood splattered on Aaron's brow."

The beginning of a genre manuscript should include the following five elements:

1. A hook. Some ideas for good beginning sentences include those containing a question, an intriguing situation, a dilemma, a conflict, or a dangerous element. In other words, something that will catch the reader's interest, pique his curiosity, and evoke anticipation regarding the solution. Less effective ways of starting a story include describing the weather, relating the history of the setting or the protagonist, or referring to everything being status quo. It's also important to start in a scene rather than with narrative, and it's better to start in the middle of a scene than in the beginning.

2. The setting. This doesn't have to be elaborate. Just state where the action takes place, for example, an office, a park, a train, etc. Avoid having talking heads in white space.

3. Introduce the protagonist, if not in the first sentence, then at least in the first paragraph.

4. Start to build a rapport between the reader and the protagonist, which will spark interest and engagement with the character and the story.

5. Reveal the genre. Prospective readers often scan the first page to find out if the author delivers what he advertised on the cover and in blurbs.

Here's the revised first page of *The Celtic Crow Murders*. Can you identify the five elements mentioned above that the beginning paragraph contains? Notice how I removed the exposition so the scene flows better.

Aaron's death was no accident. Larissa gripped the edge of her husband's open casket and bit her lip. No matter what the police said. She glanced around the room. All the other mourners had left the funeral home. So why did she feel someone's presence?

She bent over to kiss Aaron's cheek, and a tear fell. Larissa trudged into the darkened hallway. She stood in front of an ornate mirror and dialed her daughter's number. Larissa froze at a masked man's reflection. With the phone glued to her ear, she whirled in his direction.

The man, holding a dagger and shrouded in a long black coat, loomed over the coffin. She'd have to walk past the wide doorway to escape. Her grip tightened on the phone. Where was Claire?

"Hi, Mom."

"Call the police and send them to the funeral home."

The man reached into his coat and drew out a hexagonal package. He placed it in the coffin, and then raised the dagger.

Her blood turned to ice.

He made circling motions as he lowered it until the tip reached the neck. He paused. The man chanted foreign words and then extended his left arm. He slashed his palm. Blood splattered on Aaron's brow.

Larissa opened her mouth, but no scream escaped.

The back exit was closer. She ran to the office and shoved the door. It creaked open. The mortician's wife sat in a chair facing the wall.

"Hurry, we have to get out of here!" She fumbled with the door and glanced at the woman. She hadn't moved. Around the chair blood pooled.

The man in the ski mask filled the doorway, his dagger streaked with red.

Larissa shrieked.

Chapter Seven

Character and Setting Description

Convention

The convention in genre prose regarding character and setting description involves avoiding large clumps of prose. Dense blocks of text take the reader out of the story and can interfere with moving the plot forward. And readers tend to skip over those paragraphs and gravitate toward friendlier greater-white-space dialogue and action scenes.

Character Description

It's a cliché to describe a character's appearance by having her look in a mirror and then reveal her reactions. This method also includes gazing into a lake, pond, ocean, polished brass pot, or someone's mirrored sunglasses. In other words, any reflective surface.

Less is more with description. The perspective character might note two distinctive and therefore memorable features of someone upon first meeting him. Using senses in addition to that of sight enhances reader involvement.

Rather than depending on a character's thoughts, a writer can divulge information in dialogue. With this method, characters other than the perspective character can reveal elements of description without the author's head hopping. Any character can comment on description. For a subtle way of relaying characteristics, a character might compare himself to someone else, such as referencing similarities or differences with a sibling, parent, or other relative.

Including divergent impressions from characters regarding another character can be intriguing. The reader will wonder whose impressions are accurate in addition to possibly revealing the true nature and motives of the observers.

If a number of characters have different opinions about a first-person main character compared to the ones she exhibits about herself, the conflicting impressions hint that the protagonist functions as an unreliable narrator.

Settings

As mentioned in chapter six, it's not a good idea to start a work with the description of setting, because it usually doesn't function as a hook compared to starting in the middle of a scene. A brief reference to the locale, such as office building, park, train station, etc., furnishes the information needed.

Setting description becomes more vivid when a character interacts with the environment.

Example without Interaction
The desert was dry and dusty.

Example with Interaction

Joshua, sweat dripping off his brow, kicked the desert floor. The ground erupted, and a terracotta cloud consumed him. He hacked and palmed his cheeks. Joshua wiped away moist grit and then pulled his neckerchief up. He used his nose as a peg.

Instead of describing setting in static terms using state-of-being verbs, employ active verbs. Compare "The night sky was dark" to "The night rolled out a black roof the stars pierced."

Chapter Eight

Endings and Other Possible Rejection Culprits

Endings are usually the last parts read and often remembered most. These memories are good or bad depending on the effort an author puts forth to make the finale resonant.

But writers should consider another factor. Many editors have pet peeves about endings, and the following are some of the most common.

The Dream

The it-was-all-a-dream ending ranks high as an excuse to relegate a manuscript to the reject pile. Submission guidelines often include a caveat against this type of finale.

An Animal Narrator

Some popular adult books have this type of narrator. However, it grates on many gatekeepers' nerves, often more so when the writer hides the character's true identity until the end.

Dead Person Narrator

This ending may evoke a similar response to the category above.

Unanswered Questions

Sometimes authors end a book and leave out resolutions to important problems or don't reveal what happened to key characters. Every situation doesn't have to rectify itself, and sometimes characters can go missing. But if one of the characters at some point in the story at least refers to these situations, then the lack of explanation doesn't seem as though it's just an oversight.

Lack of Resonance

Sometimes stories have an arc (setup, rising tension, climax, and resolution) that's weak and seems to drift to the end. It's as though a series of disconnected events make up the tale. And at the finale, nothing has changed, so the editor, scratching his head, rejects the manuscript.

Second-Person Point of View

Another nerve-grating element for publishers. Many people find it too obtrusive.

First-Person Sociopathic Narrator

A frequent inhabitant of editors' dislike lists.

Cruelty to Children or Animals

This category is self-explanatory. However, in the animal category, readers seem to find cruelty to cats especially distasteful.

Some Exceptions to the Rules...uh...I Mean Conventions

I transgressed some of these conventions on various occasions, but I felt strongly about the stories and that the method I chose to tell them was the best one. And they were published.

If you're going to stray from the conventions, be sure you know what they are, break them for a good reason, and ignore them with skillful writing.

And remember, a character with a strong voice is irresistible to many editors and might get a manuscript in the acceptance pile regardless of its faults.

Chapter Nine

Before You Submit...
A Checklist for Genre Writers

Improve a manuscript by considering the following elements:

- Attention-getting title

- A hook first sentence

- Protagonist introduction, empathy building, brief mention of setting, and genre disclosure included optimally in the first paragraph or at least on the first page

- Characters' names not starting with the same letters or having other similarities

- No unnecessary dialogue tags

- Specific nouns and verbs rather than description with adjectives and adverbs
- Word search for -ly adverbs
- No omitted quotation marks
- Revision of end-of-sentence prepositional phrases
- No head hopping
- Correct use of its and it's
- No unnecessary use of the word *that*
- Sentence- and paragraph-length variation
- Revision of very long paragraphs
- Word-repetition check
- Scanning for possible revision of *is, are, was,* or *were* constructions

- No filters, such as felt, thought, knew, smelled, heard, and saw

- Resonant ending

Chapter Ten

Websites

Associations

www.horror.org

The Horror Writers Association is a worldwide organization for promoting the interests of horror and dark fantasy writers.

www.mysterywriters.org

Mystery Writers of America is an organization for mystery and crime writers and readers, as well as others in allied fields.

www.rwa.org

Romance Writers of America is an association for romance writers and related industry professionals.

www.sfwa.org

Science Fiction and Fantasy Writers of America is a professional organization for authors of science fiction, fantasy, and related genres. The section called Writer Beware® has information on writer scams.

Markets

www.duotrope.com

Paid subscription necessary for extensive market search engine. Subscribers also may receive a weekly e-mail with information on new and defunct markets, editorial interviews, and upcoming themed deadlines. Monthly summary edition available for nonpaid subscribers.

www.pred-ed.com

This Preditors and Editors website has resources and caveats for writers, composers, game designers, and artists.

www.ralan.com

Spec fiction (horror, science fiction, and fantasy) and humor markets. Additional useful information.

Other Writing Websites

www.savvyauthors.com

Supportive and upbeat atmosphere for writers. Informative articles. Subscription and free sections. Inexpensive classes, discounted for paid members. Learn all aspects of writing and promoting.

www.absolutewrite.com

Much here of interest to writers. The forums are very good.

www.critters.org

An excellent online critique workshop.

http://hiveword.com/wkb/search?q=voice

Writers Knowledge Base is a search engine for writing information.

Software for Writers

http://www.literatureandlatte.com

Scrivener is an inexpensive and valuable tool for managing writing projects. It even has a virtual corkboard that holds notes on book sections. Free trial download.

Patricia La Barbera, MFA, is an author and editor who specializes in genre categories. She also teaches writing and judges contests. Various journals and anthologies have published her short stories and poetry. She organized the Sarasota Editors Association and lives in Florida with her husband. Learn more about Patricia's editing services by visiting www.patricialabarbera.com. To schedule writing classes or editing, email to the following address: editor@patricialabarbera.com.

Other Books by the Author

The Celtic Crow Murders

The Wolf's Daughter (The Tala Chronicles, Book 1)

The Wolf's Revenge (The Tala Chronicles, Book 2)

Wolf Slayer (The Tala Chronicles, Book 3)

Printed in Great Britain
by Amazon